AF259326

KEBAB

AND

SHISH RECIPES

CONTENTS

INTRODUCTION

This cookbook is a compilation of your favorite kebab and shish recipes which are simply delicious, nutritious and flavour-packed. Do you know what is more? These recipes are known to serve as the tastiest dinner and lunch recipes, covered/designed with sweet and juicy sauces and marinades that brings cravings to the dining tables. You can never get enough. This cookbook will take you through a journey of flavourful, colourful, and marinated steak, beef, chicken, lamb, fish, and pork kebab recipes with quarters of fresh vegetables.

DELICIOUS KEBAB AND SHISH RECIPES

BRAZILIAN STEAK AND CHICKEN KEBABS

Prep/cooking time: 20 minutes

Serving yield: 6

INGREDIENTS

1. 1 package of steak marinade (Grill Mates Brazilian).
2. 1/4 cup of water.
3. 1/4 cup of oil.
4. 1 tablespoon of apple cider vinegar.
5. 1 1/2 pounds of your preferred steak and chicken.
6. 1 sliced/cut red bell pepper.
7. 1 chunk cut green bell pepper.
8. Finely chopped cilantro.

INSTRUCTIONS

1. Using a large mixing bowl, add in the steak marinade, water, oil, and vinegar then mix properly to combine. In a large zip lock bag, add in the sliced chicken, steak, and the marinade, shake to coat then marinate for about thirty minutes in the refrigerator.
2. Next, take the meat out of the marinade, discard the marinade then thread the chicken, beef, and vegetables alternately onto the skewers then set aside. Preheat a grill to medium-high, add the kebab on top of the grill and grill for about ten to fifteen minutes until the beef and chicken is cooked through.
3. Make sure the veggies are crisp-tender as well. Add some sprinkles of cilantro on top then serve with lemon wedges. Enjoy.

NUTRITIONAL CONTENTS

Calories 400.0, Fat 5.6 g, Carbohydrate 20.4 g, Fiber 6.4 g, and Protein 38.4 g

DELICIOUS TURKISH LAMB KEBABS

Prep/cooking time: 50 Minutes

Serving yield: 6-8

INGREDIENTS

Kebabs

1. 800g of lamb mince.
2. 1 tablespoon of dried chili flakes.
3. 4 teaspoons of sumac.
4. 4 teaspoons of ground cumin.
5. 4 tablespoons of chopped parsley stalks.
6. 6 crushed garlic cloves.

Sumac onions

1. 2 thinly sliced onions.

2. Chopped parsley leaves, about ½ a bunch.
3. 1 tablespoon of sumac.

INSTRUCTIONS

1. Preheat a grill or a barbeque on medium-high, using a large mixing bowl, add in all the ingredients for the kabab then mix properly to combine. Feel free to add your preferred seasonings as well.
2. Next, form about twelve lamb kebabs from the mixture then thread onto the skewers. Using a large bowl filled with iced water, add in the onions add let soak for about twenty minutes. Darin out the water, add in the rest of the ingredients including your preferred seasonings and mix.
3. Place the lamb kebab on the preheated grill and grill for about four minutes on both sides until it is cooked properly. Serve the lamb kebabs with the prepared sumac onions then serve.

NUTRITIONAL CONTENTS

Calories 224. Fat 14.1g, carbohydrates 2.9g, fiber 1.6g, and protein 20.5g.

VEGETABLE KEBABS

Prep/cooking time: 1 hour 10 minutes

Serving yield: 8

INGREDIENTS

For vinaigrette

1. 1/2 cup of white-wine vinegar.
2. 1 tablespoon of balsamic vinegar.
3. 1 large and minced garlic clove.
4. 1 1/4 teaspoons of sugar.
5. 1/2 teaspoon of salt to taste.
6. 1/4 teaspoon of black pepper to taste.
7. 1 cup of olive oil.

For vegetables

1. 1 lb. of sliced/cut small zucchini.

2. 3/4 lb. of sliced cherry tomatoes.
3. 1 lb. of sliced baby eggplant.
4. 10 oz. of trimmed mushrooms.
5. 2 yellow and sliced bell peppers.
6. 1 large and cut red onion.
7. 1/4 cup of olive oil.
8. 1 1/2 teaspoons of salt to taste.
9. 3/4 teaspoon of black pepper to taste.

INSTRUCTIONS

1. Using a large mixing bowl, add in all the ingredients for the vinaigrette then mix properly to combine, set aside. Using another bowl, add in the zucchini alongside with 2 teaspoons oil, 1/4 teaspoon salt, and 3/4 teaspoon black pepper then mix together to combine. Make sure you coat properly.
2. Repeat the same procedure with the rest of the vegetables, coating properly in oil and seasoning with salt and pepper. Thread the veggies alternately onto the skewers or you can decide to thread the veggies each on separate skewers.
3. Preheat the grill on medium-high, grease a grill rack with oil, add in the veggie kebabs and grill for about six to ten minutes until the veggies become tender and lightly brown while the tomatoes, blistered and shriveled. Once cooked, take the veggies out of the grill then unthread from the skewers.
4. Add some drizzles of the prepared vinaigrette on both sides then serve.

NUTRITIONAL CONTENTS

Calories 127, Fat 9.5g, Carbohydrate 10g, Fiber 2.3g, and Protein 2.4g

SWORDFISH KEBABS WITH GARLIC MARINADE

Prep/cooking time: 15 minutes

Serving yield: 2

INGREDIENTS

1. 2 (4 ounces) swordfish.
2. 3 peeled cloves of garlic.
3. 1/4 quartered onion.
4. 1/4 medium, stemmed, quartered, and seeded red bell pepper.

5. 1/4 cup of olive oil.
6. 1/8 cup of dry white wine.
7. 1 tablespoon of ketchup.
8. 1 tablespoon of sweet paprika.
9. 1/2 teaspoon of salt to taste.
10. 1/4 teaspoon of ground black pepper.
11. 1/8 cup of chopped cilantro.

INSTRUCTIONS

1. Use clean and running water to rinse the swordfish then dry with a paper towel. Place the swordfish in a large baking dish big enough to hold it then set aside. Using a food processor or a high-speed blender, add in ingredients like garlic, onion, bell pepper, oil, wine, ketchup, paprika, salt, and black pepper to taste then blend until mixture becomes a smooth puree.
2. Next, add in the chopped cilantro and blend again. This makes the garlic marinade. Pour the marinade into the baking dish containing the fish, turn properly to coat, cover the dish and marinate in the refrigerator for about one hour.
3. Preheat the grill to medium-high, oil the grate of the grill, thread the fish onto the skewers then place the fish steak on the grill. Grill the swordfish for about four to six minutes on each side until it becomes opaque in the center when pierced with a fork. Serve.

NUTRITIONAL CONTENTS

Calories: 145, Fat 9.2g, Carbohydrate 14.3 g, Fiber 0.0 g, and Protein 28.9 g.

DELICIOUS MEXICAN LIME CHICKEN KEBABS

Prep/cooking time: 40 minutes

Serving yield: 2

INGREDIENTS

1. 1 tablespoon of olive oil.
2. 1/2 teaspoon of ground cumin.
3. A handful of chopped fresh coriander.
4. 1/2 lime, juiced.
5. Salt and ground black pepper to taste.
6. 1 sliced/cubed skinless, boneless chicken breast fillets.
7. 1/2 small and sliced courgette.
8. 1/2 onion, cut into wedges and separated.
9. 1/2 sliced red pepper.
10. 5 cherry tomatoes.

INSTRUCTIONS

1. Using a small mixing bowl, add in ingredients like olive oil, cumin, chopped coriander, lime juice, chicken, salt, and pepper to taste then mix properly to combine. Place the chicken with its marinade in the refrigerator for about one hour to marinate.
2. Preheat the grill or barbeque on high, take the chicken out of the refrigerator and discard the marinade. Next, thread the chicken, courgette, onion, red pepper, and tomatoes onto the skewers, grease the grill grate with oil then grill the chicken and veggies for about ten minutes until the chicken is cooked through. Make sure you turn as you cook. Serve.

NUTRITIONAL CONTENTS

Calories 313.4, Fat 3.1 g, Carbohydrate 15.2 g, Fiber 0.6 g, and Protein 55.0 g

MEXICAN FAJITA KEBABS

Prep/cooking time: 20 minutes

Marinating time: 8 hours

Serving yield: 8

INGREDIENTS

1. 1/4 cup of olive oil.
2. 1/4 cup of balsamic vinegar.
3. 1/4 cup of fresh juice.
4. 3/4 teaspoon of ground cumin.
5. 1 1/2 teaspoons of dried and crushed oregano.
6. 4 minced cloves of garlic.
7. 1/4 cup of fresh and chopped cilantro.
8. 1 sliced serrano chile pepper which is optional.
9. 1 sliced/cut red bell pepper.
10. 1 sliced green or yellow bell pepper.
11. 1 medium and sliced sweet onion.
12. 2 pounds of sliced skinless, boneless chicken breast.

INSTRUCTIONS

1. Using a large zip lock bag, add in the olive oil, balsamic vinegar, lime juice, cumin, oregano, garlic, and cilantro then mix properly to combine. This makes the marinade. To the bag containing the marinade, add in the Chile pepper, bell peppers, sweet onion, and chicken then toss everything together to combine.
2. Place the chicken marinade into the refrigerator and marinate for about eight hours or preferably overnight. Preheat the grill on high, take the beef marinade out of the refrigerator, set the marinade aside for blasting then thread the beef and vegetables alternately onto the skewers.
3. Place the kebab on the preheated grill and grill for about fifteen minutes until it is cooked as desired. Don't forget to turn and blast the beef with the reserved marinade as you grill. Serve.

NUTRITIONAL CONTENTS

Calories 126, fat 7.5g; carbohydrates 4g; and protein 10.7g.

ASIAN SALMON AND PINEAPPLE KABABS

Prep/cooking time: 35 minutes

Serving yield: 2

INGREDIENTS:

1. 1 pound of sliced skinless salmon fillet.
2. 1 fresh, peeled and cut pineapple.

FOR THE MARINADE

1. 1 tablespoon of reduced-sodium soy sauce.
2. 1 tablespoon of oyster sauce.
3. 1 tablespoon of freshly grated ginger.
4. 1/2 tablespoon of seasoned rice vinegar.
5. 1/2 tablespoon of packed brown sugar.
6. 1 1/2 minced cloves of garlic.
7. 1/2 teaspoon of sesame oil.
8. 1/2 teaspoon of Sriracha which is optional.
9. Freshly ground black pepper, to taste.
10. Sesame seeds to serve.

INSTRUCTIONS

1. Using a small mixing bowl, add in all the ingredients for the marinade then mix properly to combine. Thread the salmon and pineapple alternately onto the skewers, add some brushes of the prepared marinade on both sides of the skewers then let sit for about ten to fifteen minutes.

2. Preheat the grill to medium-high heat, place the marinated salmon and pineapple kebabs on the grill and grill for about five to seven minutes until the salmon is cooked through and becomes opaque in nature. Make sure you turn and blast the kabab with marinade as you cook. Serve with some sprinkles of sesame seeds.

NUTRITIONAL CONTENTS

Calories 368.1, Fat 12.4g, Carbohydrate 27.9g, Fiber 3.3g, and Protein 36.7g.

GREEK LAMB SKEWERS

Prep/cooking time: 25 minutes

Serving yield: 4

INGREDIENTS

1. 1½ kg of lamb.
2. 100ml of olive oil.
3. 100ml of red wine.
4. 2 teaspoons of dried oregano.
5. Zest and juice of 2 lemons.
6. 2 crushed garlic cloves.

INSTRUCTIONS

1. Using a large mixing bowl, add in the lamb, olive oil, wine, oregano, lemon zest and juice, garlic and black pepper to taste them mix properly to combine. Place the lamb mixture into the refrigerator for a few hours or preferably overnight and let marinate.

2. Next, take the lamb out of the fridge, discard the marinade then thread the lamb onto the skewers then set aside. Preheat the grill on high, season the lamb kebabs with salt to taste then place them on the preheated grill.
3. Grill the lamb kebab for about ten to twelve minutes until cooked through. Make sure you turn as you cook. Serve.

NUTRITIONAL CONTENTS

Calories 356, fat 16g, carbohydrates 20g, fiber 2g, and protein 34g

TURKISH SPICY CHICKEN KEBABS

Prep/cooking time: 35 minutes

Serving yield: 4

INGREDIENTS

1. 2 garlic cloves.
2. 200g of Greek yogurt.
3. 1 lemon, juiced.
4. 2 teaspoons of tomato purée.
5. 2 teaspoons of chili flakes.
6. 2 teaspoons of sumac.
7. 4 sliced chicken breasts.
8. 300g of plum tomatoes.
9. 1 red chili.
10. 2 tablespoons of extra virgin olive oil.
11. 1 small and sliced red onion.
12. 1 tablespoon of pomegranate molasses.

INSTRUCTIONS

1. Using a large mixing bowl, add in about 1 garlic clove then crush. To the garlic, add in other ingredients like 3 tablespoons of yogurt, lemon juice, 1 teaspoon of tomato purée, half the spices, and your favorite seasonings then mix properly to combine. This makes the marinade.
2. To the marinade, add in chicken, cover the bowl and place in the fridge for about one hour or preferably overnight. To make the chili sauce, using a food processor or a high-speed blender, add in about 100g of tomatoes, red chili, the rest of the spices, garlic clove, tomato puree, a tablespoon of oil, half of the red onion, and molasses then pulse until mixture becomes smooth.
3. Preheat the oven to 400 degrees F, grease a griddle pan with oil and heat. Thread the chicken onto the skewers, use a paper towel to wipe off any excess marinade, add the kebab into prepared griddle pan and cook for a few minutes on both sides.
4. Transfer the kebab into a baking sheet, place the baking sheet into the preheated oven and bake for about ten minutes until the chicken is cooked through. You can thread the rest of the tomato on a separate skewers and cook on the griddle pan for about two minutes on both sides.
5. Serve.

NUTRITIONAL CONTENTS

Calories 276, fat 12g, carbohydrates 7g, and 6g Fiber.

SESAME AND CHICKEN KEBAB

Prep/cooking time: 25 minutes

Serving yield: 6

INGREDIENTS

1. 4 pounds of chicken tenders.
2. 6 peeled and crushed garlic cloves.
3. 1 cup of soy sauce.
4. 1/2 cup of seasoned rice wine vinegar.
5. 4 tablespoons of honey.
6. 2 tablespoons of fresh, peeled and grated ginger.
7. 6 medium and chopped green onions.
8. 4 tablespoons of toasted sesame oil.
9. 4-6 sprigs of fresh cilantro for garnish.
10. 1 lime juiced.
11. 2 teaspoons of toasted sesame seeds.

INSTRUCTIONS

1. Using a large mixing bowl, add in the soy sauce, garlic, vinegar, honey, ginger, onions, lime juice, sesame oil, and sesame seeds then mix properly to combine. this makes the marinade. Pour the prepared marinade into a plastic bag or a zip bag, add in the chicken then coat properly with the marinade.
2. Place the plastic bag into the fridge for about one to two hours to marinate properly. Once it is ready, remove the chicken from the marinade and set the marinade aside. Thread the chicken onto the skewers, add some drizzles of the marinade over the chicken skewers and let sit.
3. Preheat the grill on medium-high, place the chicken skewers on the preheated grill and grill for about three minutes. Turn the chicken skewers over and cook for an additional three minutes until it is cooked through and an inserted thermometer reads 170 degrees F. serve.

NUTRITIONAL CONTENTS

Calories 269, Fat 8g, Carbohydrates 11g, and Protein 34g

ASIAN GARLIC STEAK KEBABS

Prep/cooking time: 20 minutes

Serving yield: 6

INGREDIENTS

1. 1 1/2 pounds of sirloin steak.
2. 1 onion.
3. 2/3 cup of soy sauce.
4. 6 minced garlic cloves.
5. 1/4 cup of sesame oil.
6. ½ cup of vegetable oil.
7. ½ cup of sugar.
8. 1 tablespoon of grated ginger.
9. 2 tablespoons of sesame seeds.

INSTRUCTIONS

1. Use a sharp knife to cut the steak and onions into desired chunks then set aside. Using large mixing bowls, add in the rest of the ingredients on the list then mix properly to combine. Add the

steak into the bowl containing the marinade, toss properly to coat, cover the bowl and let marinate in the fridge for about three hours or overnight.

2. Next, preheat a grill to medium-high, threat the marinated steak and chopped/cubed onions onto the skewers then grill for about ten minutes on both sides until the steak is cooked through. Serve.

NUTRITIONAL CONTENTS

Calories 490, Fat 33g, Carbohydrates 22g, Fiber 1g, and Protein 29g.

TURKISH TURKEY KEBABS

Prep/cooking time: 45 minutes

Serving yield: 6

INGREDIENTS

1. 750 g of sliced/cut turkey breast.
2. 1 medium onion.
3. 1 teaspoon of paprika powder.
4. 1 teaspoon of dried thyme.
5. 1 teaspoon of fine sea salt and more.
6. 1/2 teaspoon of ground black pepper for taste.
7. 3 tablespoons of rice or cider vinegar as desired.
8. 2 tablespoons of extra virgin olive oil.
9. 1 sliced/cut small zucchini.
10. 1 sliced cherry tomatoes.
11. 1 yellow and sliced bell peppers.

INSTRUCTIONS

1. Properly grate the onions into a large mixing bowl, add in other ingredients like the sweet paprika, thyme, salt, pepper, vinegar, and olive oil then mix properly to combine. this actually makes the marinade. Use a sharp kitchen knife to cut the turkey into desired shapes, add the turkey into the bowl containing the marinade then toss properly to coat.
2. Next, cover the turkey marinade with a plastic wrap, place in the refrigerator and marinate for about two hours. Thread the turkey and veggies onto the skewers, brush the surface of the turkey skewers with oil then add some sprinkles of salt to taste.
3. Next, preheat the grill on medium-high, brush the grill grate with oil then place the turkey skewers on it. Grill the turkey kebab for about fifteen minutes on both sides until it is fully cooked. Make sure you turn as you cook. Serve.

NUTRITIONAL CONTENTS

Calories: 239, fat: 7g, carbohydrates: 3g, fiber: 0g, and protein: 38g.

CHICKEN SHISH KEBOBS

Prep/cooking time: 25 minutes

Serving yield: 6

INGREDIENTS

1. 2 lbs. of cubed chicken breast.
2. 3 tablespoons of lemon juice.
3. 1 tablespoon of olive oil.
4. 2 chopped cloves of garlic.
5. 1/4 teaspoon of cumin.
6. 1/2 teaspoon of pepper.
7. 1/8 teaspoon of cayenne.
8. 1 sliced/cut small zucchini.
9. 1 sliced cherry tomatoes.
10. 1 yellow and sliced bell peppers.
11. 1 sliced red onion.

INSTRUCTIONS

1. Using a large mixing bowl, add in all the ingredients on the list then mix properly to combine. let the mixture sit for about two hours to overnight in the refrigerator to properly marinate. Next, Remove the chicken from its marinade, thread each chicken with the sliced veggies onto the skewers then set aside.
2. Preheat the grill to medium-high, oil the grates of the grill then place the chicken shish on it. Grill the chicken shish for about fifteen minutes until it is cooked through while turning at intervals. Serve.

NUTRITIONAL CONTENTS

Calories 306, fat 17g, carbohydrates 6g, and protein 31g.

DELICIOUS BRAZILIAN STEAK KEBABS

Prep/cooking time: 52

Serving yield: 8

INGREDIENTS

Kabobs

1. 1 1/2 lbs. of sliced/cut sirloin steak.
2. 1 sliced red bell pepper.
3. 1 sliced green bell pepper.
4. 1 large and sliced onion.
5. Salt and pepper to taste.

Marinade

1. 1 pkg. of Brazilian Steakhouse Marinade.
2. 1/4 cup of olive oil.
3. 2 tablespoons of low sodium soy sauce.
4. 2 tablespoons of Worcestershire sauce.
5. 1 tablespoon of lime juice.

INSTRUCTIONS

1. In other to make the marinade, place all the ingredients in a large mixing bowl then mix properly to combine. reserve about one cup of marinade then asset aside for blasting the veggies when grilling. Add the sliced steak into the bowl containing the marinade them toss to coat.
2. Place the steak marinade in the refrigerator for about four to six minutes to marinate properly. You can cook the potatoes with about two tablespoons of water in a microwave for about four to five minutes until it becomes tender, set aside.
3. In another mixing bowl, add in about two tablespoons of the reserved marinade, peppers, onions, 2 tablespoons of olive oil, 1/2 teaspoon salt, and 1/4 pepper to taste then mix to combine. place the veggie marinade into the refrigerator for a few minutes to marinade.
4. Preheat a grill to medium-high then grease, thread the steak and veggies alternately onto the skewers then grill for about two to three minutes on both sides until it is cooked through. Make sure you turn and blast the kebab with the rest of the marinade as you grill. Serve.

NUTRITIONAL CONTENTS

Calories 182, Fat 14g, Carbohydrates 2g, Fiber 0.5g, and Protein 13g.

DELICIOUS PORK SKEWERS

Prep/cooking time: 40

Serving yield: 10

INGREDIENTS

1. 900g of pre-cooked pork belly.
2. 6 tablespoons of dark soy sauce.
3. 4 tablespoons of fish sauce.
4. 1 tablespoon of grated ginger.
5. 2 limes, juiced
6. 175g of soft brown sugar.
7. 1 chopped red chili.

INSTRUCTIONS

1. use a sharp knife to cut the pork into smaller cubes then set aside. Place a saucepan over medium-low heat, add in other ingredients like soy sauce, fish sauce, ginger, lime juice, and brown sugar then mix to combine. let the mixture heat up for about a few minutes until it bubbles. Make sure you stir as you cook.

2. Once heated, let the mixture cool then set aside. This makes the marinade. reserve a little portion of the marinade, add the sliced/cubed pork into the bowl containing the marinade then toss properly to combine.

3. Place the pork marinade into the fridge and let it marinate for about thirty minutes. Next, add the chili to the reserved marinade, mix properly to combine then set aside. This makes the dipping sauce. Next, preheat the oven to 400 degrees F, place parchment paper on a baking tray then set aside.

4. Thread the pork onto the skewers, place them on the lined baking tray and cook for about twenty minutes until they become golden in colour, sticky and caramelized. Serve the pork skewers with the prepared sauce, enjoy.

NUTRITIONAL CONTENTS

Calories 369, fat 21.1g, carbohydrates 18.6g, fiber 0.3g, and protein 26g

GRILLED THAI CURRY CHICKEN KEBABS

Prep/cooking time: 40 Minutes

Serving yield: 3

INGREDIENTS

For the chicken

1. 1/3 cup of soy sauce.
2. 2 tablespoons of dark brown sugar.
3. Zest of one lime.
4. 1 tablespoon of vegetable oil.
5. 2 minced garlic cloves.
6. 1/2 tablespoon of curry powder.
7. 1/4 teaspoon of ground ginger.
8. 1/4 teaspoon of ground cardamom.
9. 1/4 teaspoon of salt to taste.
10. 2 pounds of boneless, skinless chicken breasts.

For the coconut-peanut sauce

1. 1 (13-oz) can of coconut milk.
2. 1/8 cup of peanut butter.
3. 1/3 cup of dark brown sugar.

4. 1/2 tablespoon of soy sauce.
5. 1/2 tablespoon of red curry paste.
6. 2 tablespoons of fresh lime juice, from 2 limes

For serving

1. 1 lime, cut into wedges (optional)

INSTRUCTIONS

1. Using a large kitchen knife, cut the chicken into smaller pieces then set aside. Using a large mixing bowl, add in ingredients like soy sauce, dark brown sugar, lime zest, vegetable oil, garlic, curry powder, ginger, cardamom, and salt to taste then mix properly to combine. This makes the marinade.
2. Add the chicken pieces into the bowl containing the marinade then toss to coat. Cover the chicken marinade with a plastic wrap and marinate in the refrigerator for about four hours, preferably overnight.
3. In other to make the sauce, add in all its ingredients (aside from the lime juice) into a mixing bowl then mix properly to combine. Place a saucepan over medium heat, pour in the mixed ingredients then simmer for about three minutes. Don't forget to stir as you cook. Add in the juice then set the sauce aside.
4. Preheat a grill to medium-high, grease the grill, thread the chicken onto the skewers and grill the chicken kebabs for about ten minutes until it is cooked through. Only turn once. Serve the grilled curry chicken with the prepared sauce and enjoy.

NUTRITIONAL CONTENTS

Calories:547, Fat:29 g, Carbohydrates:21 g, Fiber:2 g, and Protein:52 g.

DELICIOUS SAUSAGE KEBABS

Prep/cooking time: 20 minutes

Serving yield: 4

INGREDIENTS

1.   vegetable oil for frying
2.   About 20 cocktail sausages.
3.   1 tablespoon of honey.
4.   ½ tablespoon of rose harissa.
5.   1/2 tablespoon of orange juice.
6.   1/4 teaspoon of ground cinnamon.

Veggies

1.   1 sliced/cut small zucchini.
2.   1 sliced cherry tomatoes.
3.   1 yellow and sliced bell peppers.
4.   1 sliced red onion.

INSTRUCTIONS

1. Place a frying pan over medium-high heat then add in the oil. Once the oil is hot, thread the sausages and all the vegetables onto a skewers, add in the sausages skewers and cook for a few minutes until they are completely cooked through. Make sure you turn until the sausages become brown in colour.
2. Using a large mixing bowl, add in the rest of the ingredients on the list then mix properly to combine. Pour the mixed ingredients into the pan containing the sausages and vegetables and cook for a few more minutes until it becomes sticky. Serve.

NUTRITIONAL CONTENTS

Calories 240, Fat 17.7g, Carbohydrates 11.4g, Fiber 2.1g, and Protein 7.9g

SRIRACHA AND LIME CHICKEN KEBABS

Prep/cooking time: 30 minutes

Serving yield: 4

INGREDIENTS

1. 3 tablespoons of Greek yogurt.
2. 3 finely chopped thyme sprigs.
3. 1 lime, ½ zested, ½ juiced.
4. 2 tablespoons of sriracha.
5. 1/4 coriander.
6. 1 tablespoon of olive oil.
7. 1/2 teaspoon of ground black peppercorns.
8. 400g of chicken mini fillets.

INSTRUCTIONS

1. Using a large mixing bowl, add in all the ingredients on the list aside from the chicken then mix properly to combine. This makes the marinade. Add the chicken fillets into the bowl containing the marinade then toss to combine.

2. Cover the chicken marinade then place into the refrigerator to marinate for about two to three hours. Thread the chicken onto a skewer then set aside. Place a grill pan over medium-high heat, add in chicken skewers and cook for about three to four minutes on both sides.
3. Serve.

NUTRITIONAL CONTENTS

Calories 195, Fat 8g, Carbohydrates 2.6g, Fiber 0.2g, and Protein 27.9g

LAMB SHISH DELIS

Prep/cooking time: 10 minutes

Serving yield: 4

INGREDIENTS

1. 600g of lamb steaks.
2. 1 tablespoon of jerk paste or marinade as desired.
3. Zest and juice of 1 lime.
4. 1/2 tablespoons of honey.
5. A handful of chopped thyme leaves.
6. 1 sliced red bell pepper.
7. 1 sliced onions.

INSTRUCTIONS

1. Using a sharp kitchen knife, dice the lamb steak into smaller pieces then add to a large mixing bowl alongside with other ingredients jerk paste, lime zest and juice, honey, thyme leaves,

and desired seasonings then mix everything to combine. Let the lamb marinate for a few hours in the refrigerator before grilling.
2. Thread the lamb, onions, and bell pepper onto a skewer then set aside. Place a griddle pan over medium-high heat, add in chicken skewers and cook for about two to three minutes on both sides until the meat is charred.
3. Once cooked, place the lamb in a foil paper and let it rest for about five minutes, serve.

NUTRITIONAL CONTENTS

Calories 258, fat 14g, carbohydrates 3g, fiber 0g, protein 29g

CHICKEN TENDERS SHISH KEBAB

Prep/cooking time: 1 hour

Serving yield: 3

INGREDIENTS

1. 1 lemon, ½ juiced, ½ cut into wedges to serve.
2. 90g of natural yogurt.
3. 2 chopped garlic cloves.
4. 1 green chili.
5. A small pack of fresh coriander.
6. 1/4 teaspoon of turmeric.
7. 1/2 teaspoon of ground cumin.
8. 1/2 teaspoon of garam masala
9. 8 skinless, boneless chicken thighs.

INSTRUCTIONS

1. Using a large mixing bowl or a high-speed blender, add in all the ingredients on the list aside from the chicken and lemon wedges then blend until mixture becomes smooth. This makes the

marinade. Using a large mixing bowl, add in chicken, pour over the prepared marinade then toss to coat.
2. Next, cover the marinade and let the chicken marinate for about four hours to two days. Preheat a grill or barbeque over medium heat, thread the chicken onto the skewers and grill on the preheated grill for about fourth-five to fifty minutes until the chicken is cooked through. Don't forget to turn as you grill.
3. Serve the kebab with any salad of choice and lemon wedges.

NUTRITIONAL CONTENTS

Calories 299, fat 19g, carbohydrates 3g, fiber 0g, and protein 29g.

ASIAN SALMON, TOMATO AND MUSHROOM KEBABS

Prep/cooking time: 35 minutes

Serving yield: 4

INGREDIENTS

Marinade:

1. 1 tablespoon of soy sauce.
2. 1 tablespoon of tomato purée.
3. Finely grated rind and juice of 1 lime.
4. 1 tablespoon of oil.
5. 1/2 tablespoon of honey.
6. ½ teaspoon of Thai fish sauce.
7. 1/4 teaspoon of chili flakes.
8. 1 tablespoon of chopped and fresh coriander.

Other ingredients:

1. 259g of firm fish fillet as desired.
2. 4 sliced mushrooms.

3.   2 Roma tomatoes.

4.   A Pinch of ground nutmeg

5.   Salt and pepper, to taste.

INSTRUCTIONS

1.   Using a large mixing bowl, add in all the ingredients for the marinade alongside with fish fillets then mix properly to combine. Cover the fish marinade with a plastic wrap and let marinate for about fifteen to thirty minutes.

2.   Thread the fish, mushrooms, and tomato onto the skewers, season with nutmeg, salt, and pepper to taste then set aside. Place a griddle pan over medium heat then add in the fish kebabs. Cook the fish and mushrooms for about five to seven minutes until it is cooked through. Don't forget to turn once as you cook. Serve.

NUTRITIONAL CONTENTS

Calories:547, Fat:29 g, Carbohydrates:21 g, Fiber:2 g, and Protein:52 g.

DELICIOUS STEAK SHISH KABOB WITH VEGGIES

Prep/cooking time: 35 minutes

Serving yield: 8

INGREDIENTS

1. 2 lb. of sliced beef steak.

For the marinade

2. 3/4 cup of soy sauce.
3. 2/3 cup of oil- preferably olive oil.
4. 1/3 cup of plain yogurt.
5. 1 teaspoon of Worcestershire sauce.
6. 1 tablespoon of white vinegar.
7. 1/4 cup of lemon juice.
8. 2 minced garlic cloves.
9. 1/2 tablespoon of yellow mustard.
10. 1 teaspoon of freshly ground black pepper.
11. 1 teaspoon of ground cardamom.

12. 1/2 teaspoon of ground cinnamon.

Veggies

1. Sliced bell peppers.
2. 5 oz. of pearl onions.
3. 8 small mushroom caps.
4. Cherry tomatoes.

INSTRUCTIONS

1. Using a large mixing bowl, add in all the ingredients for the marinade then mix properly to combine. This makes the marinade. Reserve about a half cup of marinade then pour the rest into a zip lock bag. Add in the sliced meat, toss properly to combine then place the meat marinade into the refrigerator to marinate for a few hours to overnight.
2. Slice the vegetables with a sharp knife, add them into the bowl containing the reserved marinade them mix properly to combine. Let the veggies marinate for about one hour. Thread the meat and veggies alternately onto the skewers then grill for a few minutes on both sides until the meat and veggies are cooked through. Serve.

NUTRITIONAL CONTENTS

Calories 643, Fat 36.3g, Carbohydrates 4.2g, Fiber 0.3g, and Protein 71.3g.

TERIYAKI SHISH KABABS

Prep/cooking time: 25 minutes

Serving yield: 4

INGREDIENTS

1. 1/2 cup of sugar.
2. 1/2 cup of reduced-sodium soy sauce.
3. 1/2 cup of ketchup.
4. 1 teaspoon of garlic powder.
5. 1 teaspoon of ground ginger.
6. 1 pound of sliced beef sirloin steak.
7. 1/2 sliced large green or sweet red pepper.
8. 1/2 sliced small onion.

INSTRUCTIONS

1. Using a large mixing bowl, add in the sugar, soy sauce, ketchup, garlic powder, and ginger then mix properly to combine. This actually makes the marinade. Pour the marinade into a plastic

bag, add in the beef steak, shake very well to coat then place in the refrigerator to marinate overnight.

2. Thread the sirloin steak and veggies onto the skewers then set aside. Preheat a grill to medium-high, place the steak and veggie skewers on the preheated grill and grill for about twelve to fifteen minutes until it is cooked through.

3. You can serve the kebab as it is or remove the veggies and meat from the skewers and serve on a plate.

NUTRITIONAL CONTENTS

306 calories, 5g fat, 38g carbohydrate, 2g fiber, and 27g protein.

BEEF SHISH KEBABS

Prep/cooking time: 25 minutes

Serving yield: 6

INGREDIENTS

1. 1 tablespoon of olive oil.
2. 1 teaspoon of chopped fresh rosemary.
3. 3 minced garlic cloves.
4. 1 pound of beef tenderloin.
5. 1/2 teaspoon of kosher salt.
6. 1/2 teaspoon of freshly ground black pepper.
7. 2 teaspoons of fresh lemon juice.
8. 2 cups of cherry tomatoes.
9. 1 large and diced red onion.
10. 1 s iced yellow bell pepper.

INSTRUCTIONS

1. In other to make the marinade, using a large mixing bowl, add in the oil, rosemary, and garlic them mix properly to combine. Reserve about 1/4 cup of the marinade, add the sliced beef into the bowl containing the rest of the marinade, cover the bowl

with plastic wrap and marinate in the refrigerator for about one hour.

2. To the reserved marinade, add in the veggies and marinate for about one hour. Next, take the beef and veggies out of their respective marinade, discard the marinade then thread the beef and veggies onto the skewers. Add some sprinkles of salt and pepper to taste, about ¼ teaspoon each.
3. Preheat a grill over medium-high heat, add the beef and veggie skewers and grill for about nine minutes on both sides until it is cooked through. Serve.

NUTRITIONAL CONTENTS

Calories 156, Fat 6.2g, Protein 17.1g, Carbohydrate 8.9g, and Fiber 1.8g.

BEEF AND LAMB KABABS

Prep/cooking time: 23 minutes

Serving yield: 8

INGREDIENTS

1. 1 medium, peeled, and grated onion.
2. 1/2 lb. of lean ground lamb.
3. 1/2 lb. of lean ground beef.
4. 4 chopped cloves of garlic.
5. 2 tablespoons of finely chopped parsley.
6. 1 teaspoon of kosher salt to taste.
7. 1/2 teaspoon of ground black pepper to serve.
8. 1 teaspoon of ground turmeric.
9. 1 teaspoon of paprika.
10. Ground sumac which optional.
11. 1 lemon which is optional.

INSTRUCTIONS

1. Using a large mixing bowl, add in the ground beef, lamb, shredded onions, garlic, parsley, kosher salt, pepper, turmeric, and paprika them mix properly to combine. Make about eight

shapes out of the meat mixture then thread them onto the skewers then set aside.

2. Preheat the grill to high-heat, grease the grill then place the skewers on the grill. Grill the ground meat for about three to four minutes on both sides until the meat becomes brown and cooked through.

3. Once cooked, let the meat kebab rest for about five minutes, add some sprinkles of sumac or lemon juice and serve.

NUTRITIONAL CONTENTS

Calories: 13, and Carbohydrates: 3g.

CONCLUSION

This cookbook will drive you through a part of simply amazing, delicious and satisfying recipes make with the top-notch skewers. These recipes are easy to make, nutritious, colourful, and flavour-packed. Believe me, grilling couldn't be more exciting. It's easy, get this Kebab and Shish recipes book, get your ingredients, and get the grill rolling. There isn't a better way to spend the summer.

www.ingramcontent.com/pod-product-compliance
Lightning Source LLC
Chambersburg PA
CBHW071518030726
47593CB00003B/1318